GUSTAV KLIMT
COLORING BOOK

DURING HIS LIFETIME, Gustav Klimt (Austrian, 1862–1918) was said to have created the most beautiful painting in the world. Not all critics agreed with that opinion, but one thing is certain: Gustav Klimt displayed great flair for originality in the numerous sketches and paintings he created. Whether his subjects were buildings, chickens, or people, Klimt made each image unique and striking—often by including colorful patterns and dazzling details.

You will find twenty-two of Gustav Klimt's artworks in this coloring book. They are shown as small pictures on the inside front and back covers. When you color in the line drawings, you could copy the originals or you might prefer to create your own color combinations. We've left the last page of this coloring book blank so that you can draw and color a picture of your own. Will it be a portrait, a landscape, a picture of your house and family, or something wholly from your imagination?

Pomegranate

Pomegranate Communications, Inc.
19018 NE Portal Way, Portland OR 97230
800 227 1428   www.pomegranate.com

Pomegranate Europe Ltd.
Unit 1, Heathcote Business Centre, Hurlbutt Road
Warwick, Warwickshire CV34 6TD, UK
[+44] 0 1926 430111
sales@pomeurope.co.uk

© 2010 Pomegranate Communications, Inc.

Catalog No. CB126

Designed and rendered by Susan Koop

Printed in Korea

23 22 21 20 19 18 17 16 15   13 12 11 10 9 8 7 6 5

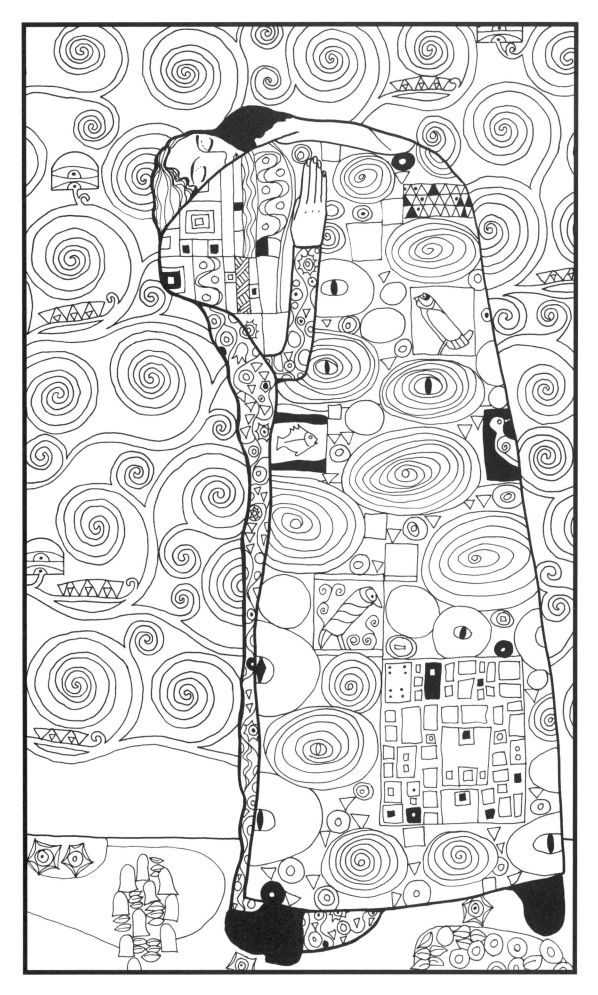

1. Design for the Stoclet frieze

2. Lady with Hat and Feather Boa

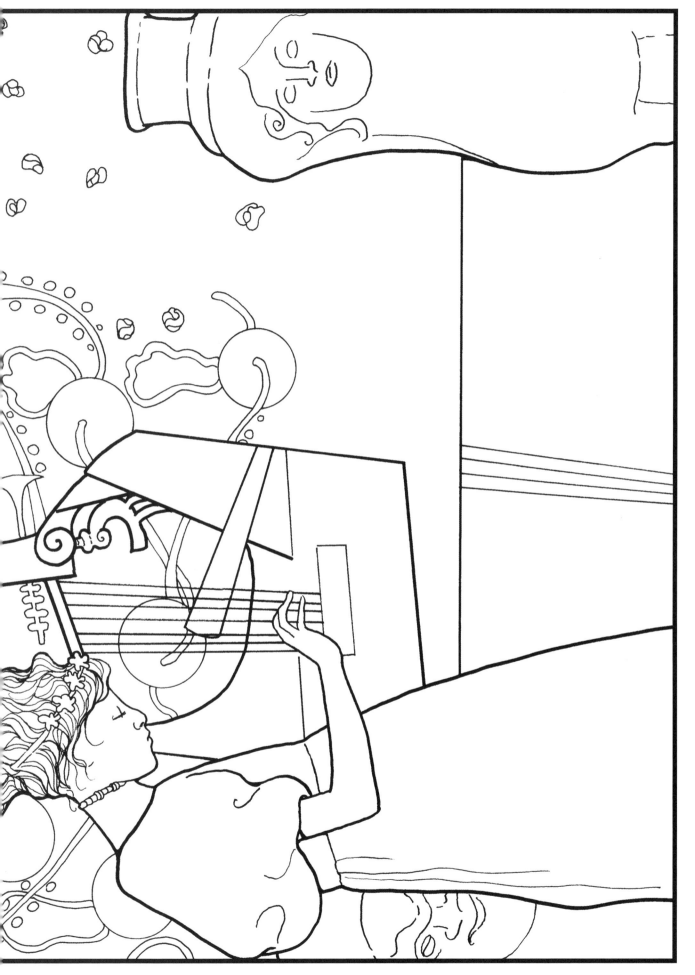

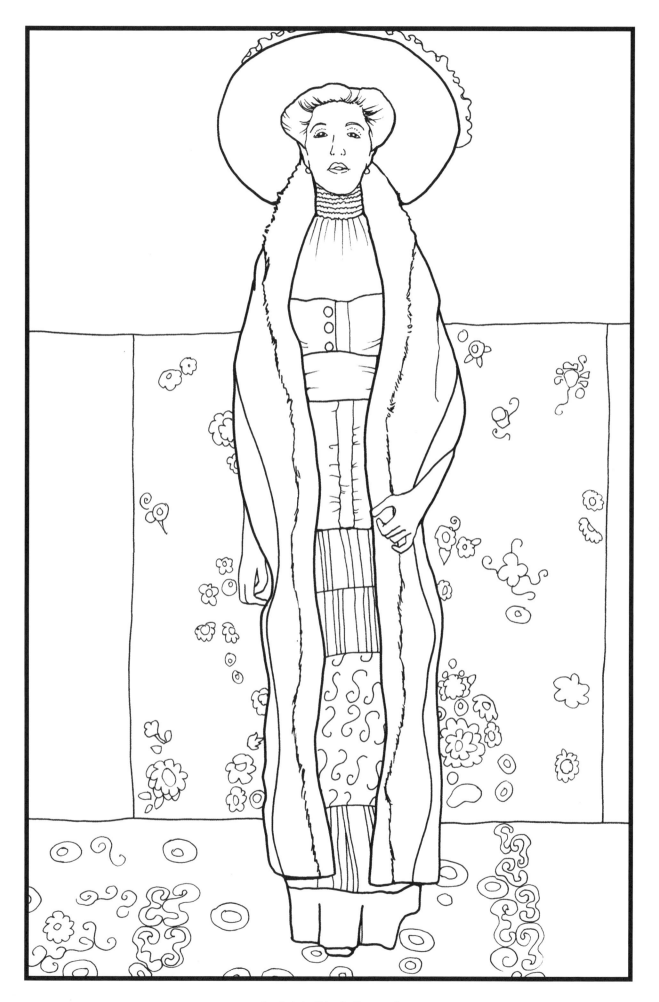

4. Adele Bloch-Bauer II

5. *Unterach Manor on the Attersee Lake, Austria* (detail)

6. *Eugenia Primavesi*

7. Sunflowers (detail)

8. *Woman with Fan* (detail)

9. *Garden Path with Hens* (detail)

10. Design for the Stoclet frieze

11. *Emilie Flöge* (detail)

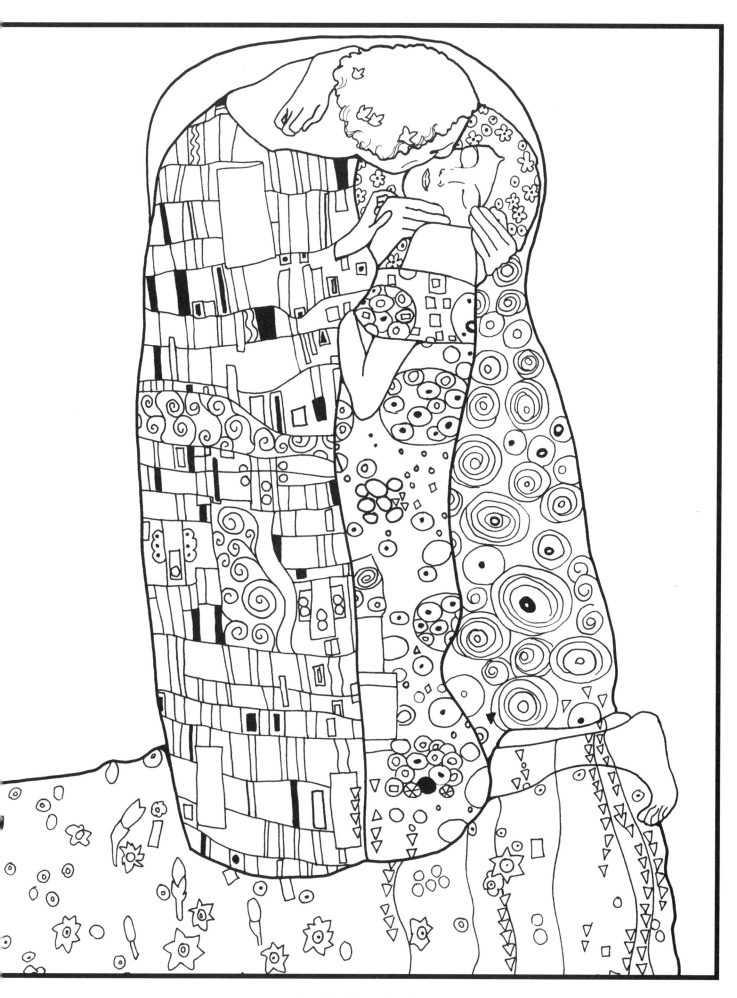

12. *The Kiss* (detail)

13. *Church in Unterach on the Attersee*

14. *Fritza Riedler* (detail)

15. *Elisabeth Bachofen-Echt*

16. Design for the Stoclet frieze (detail)

17. *Life Is a Struggle* or *The Golden Knight*

18. Friederike Maria Beer

19. Design for the Stoclet frieze (detail)

20. Johanna Staude

21. *Malcesine on Lake Garda* (detail)

22. Design for the Stoclet frieze (detail)

w and color your own picture here!